# TREASURE HUNTERS

## THE SEARCH FOR

# TOMBS

PALENQUE

SIPAN

*ATLANTIC OCEAN*

NEWGRANGE

GLASTONBURY

OSEBERG

SUTTON HOO

ÖTZTAL ALPS

MYCENAE

ROME

HALICARNASSUS

PETRA

THE VALLEY OF
THE KINGS

MANCHENG

XI'AN

PACIFIC
OCEAN

INDIAN
OCEAN

# TREASURE HUNTERS

## THE SEARCH FOR

# TOMBS

ANITA GANERI

**RSVP**

**RAINTREE**
**STECK-VAUGHN**
PUBLISHERS
The Steck-Vaughn Company

*Austin, Texas*

*For Nicky, A.G.*

Published by Raintree Steck-Vaughn Publishers, an imprint of Steck-Vaughn Company

*Concept Designer:* Jane Hannath
*Designer and Typesetter:* Kudos
*Illustrator:* Colin Sullivan
*Map Illustrator:* Bruce Hogarth
*Commissioning Editor:* Fiona Courtenay-Thompson
*Assistant Editor:* Lisa Edwards
*Series Editor:* Nicola Barber

*Photograph Acknowledgments:* AKG photo p.26(c); Sue Cunningham/SCP p.39(cb); C M Dixon p.21(tr); e.t.archive p.9(br); Mary Evans Picture Library p.22(c); Robert Harding Picture Library p.15(tl), 16(c), 29(tr), 30/31(b), 31(tr), 36(ct) 42(cl); Michael Holford p.9(c), 12(tl), 18(br), 19(br), 34(cr), 35(tr); Römisch Germanische Zentral Museum p.11(bl), (br); Peter Sanders p.25(br); The Slide File p.41(tl); Frank Spooner Pictures p.28(cb); Werner Forman Archive p.9(tr), 32(bl), 33(tr), 38(cr)

*Picture Researcher:* Shelley Noronha

### Library of Congress Cataloging-in-Publication Data

Ganeri, Anita, 1961–
    The search for tombs / Anita Ganeri.
       p.  cm. — (Treasure hunters)
    Includes bibliographical references and index.
    Summary: Discusses the discovery of notable tombs around the world, including the pyramid chamber of the Egyptian boy king Tutankhamen, the royal tombs of China, and the burial ships of Vikings.
    ISBN 0-8172-4839-0
    1. Tombs—Juvenile literature. [1. Tombs. 2. Archaeology.]
    I. Title. II. Series: Treasure hunters (Austin, Tex.)
CC77.B8G36 1998
393'.1—dc21                    96-51660
                                  CIP
                                   AC

Printed in Hong Kong by Wing King Tong
1 2 3 4 5 6 7 8 9 HK 01 00 99 98 97

# CONTENTS

# INTRODUCTION

In preparation for a life after death, people in the ancient world often buried their dead rulers in elaborate tombs, surrounded by treasures and personal possessions. Hidden from human eyes for centuries, many of these tombs and their fabulous treasures have come to light once more, providing us with a fascinating insight into how people lived and died in ancient times. For tales of great adventure, of curses and coincidences, and of dreams come true, read on . . .

In the Hindu religion, the dead are cremated on funeral pyres. Their ashes are then scattered in the sacred Ganges River.

## BURIAL CUSTOMS

Throughout the world, people have developed different ways of dealing with their dead. Their customs reflect their beliefs about what happens to people after they die. In some cultures dead people are burned, or cremated. The sacred fire of the funeral pyre is believed to carry their spirits to heaven. The Parsis of India, on the other hand, neither bury nor cremate their dead, to avoid polluting the earth or the sacred fire. Instead the corpse is taken to a huge, circular building called a tower of silence. There it is laid out in the open and left for the vultures to devour.

### Grave goods

Many people bury their dead in graves or tombs. Some of the grandest tombs of ancient times were built for mighty leaders and wealthy rulers. Such people were often buried with their most precious possessions to take with them into the next world. These possessions could include priceless treasures, weapons, armor, and furniture. Some tombs were painted with scenes from the dead person's life.

# Secrets of the tomb

Precious gold and silver items are not the only kinds of treasure found in tombs. The tombs themselves have given scholars a vast and invaluable source of information about the past. Many things are ordinary, household objects, showing how people lived, cooked, farmed, and hunted. Even the poorest people were often buried with a cooking pot or a hunting spear. By examining these goods, we can tell what people ate, what they wore, and how they prepared for death. Unfortunately many ancient tombs were looted long ago by grave robbers and unscrupulous treasure hunters, and their most precious contents were stolen. Fortunately there are still many more tombs waiting to be found.

A gold pot *(right)* from an Etruscan (Italian) tomb, dating from the 7th century BC, and exquisite jewelry *(far right)* from the royal tombs of Ur, in Sumeria, dating from about 2500 BC.

## MOVING BODIES

*Over 3,000 years ago, under cover of night, a group of priests crept into the Valley of the Kings in Egypt. In this valley were buried more than 30 rulers of Ancient Egypt. The priests broke into the tombs and removed the royal bodies. They carried the bodies and many of the treasures buried with them along a cliff-top path and out of the valley to a new and secret resting place—a cave at the bottom of a great shaft in the rocks. This was the priests' last attempt at tricking the grave robbers who had plundered the tombs for centuries. For 3,000 years the plan worked. Then, in the 1880s, priceless tomb treasures began to appear on Egyptian markets. The authorities traced the treasures to the secret cave. There they found the bodies of Egypt's greatest pharaohs, still lying in neat rows.*

The Ancient Egyptians put wooden figures of the gods in tombs in order to protect the dead.

9

# PREHISTORIC GRAVES

The custom of burying dead people in graves and performing some sort of funeral service probably began about 400,000 years ago. Rather than leaving bodies where they fell—at the mercy of wild animals or the wind and rain—prehistoric people began to use caves as ready-made tombs. Later they built more elaborate structures as graves. However, one ancient traveler was not so fortunate. His grave was an Alpine glacier. There he lay, entombed in ice, for more than 5,000 years. This is his story.

The site where Ötzi's body was discovered in 1991, near the Ötztal Valley that gave him his name.

## THE MAN IN THE ICE

On September 19, 1991, two German tourists, Helmut and Erika Simon, were returning from a long hike in the Alps close to the border between Austria and Italy. As they came down the mountain, they noticed a head and shoulders jutting out of the ice. The couple thought they had stumbled across the body of a missing climber, caught in a recent avalanche. In fact they had discovered something far more extraordinary—the body of a prehistoric man.

Ötzi's body was trapped in the ice when it was discovered by two hikers.

## Star status

Attempts were made to free the body from its icy grave. Unfortunately, as the rescuers tried to haul the man out with ice axes and ski poles, they destroyed what was left of his clothing, snapped his hunting bow, and left a gaping hole in his hip. They, like the Simons, thought that they were digging out an avalanche victim. None of them had any inkling of just how wrong they were.

More bungling followed before the body was finally taken to the University of Innsbruck. There scientists quickly realized the importance of the find, and the body was safely stored in a freezer to prevent further decay. The man was nicknamed Ötzi, after the Ötztal Valley near where he died. Within months he had become a national celebrity, with Ötzi T-shirts, postcards, and even Ötzi songs.

## Examining the evidence

Ötzi's body was taken out of the freezer for only 20 minutes at a time for brief examinations by scientists. Their findings were even more remarkable than they had dared hope.

For 5,000 years, Ötzi's body had lain in a rocky, snow-filled hollow, slightly away from the main glacier. This explained its good condition—even the man's brain and eyeballs were intact—because bodies caught in glaciers are often crushed and broken as the ice moves down the mountainside. From the style of copper axe that Ötzi carried, the scientists confirmed that he must have lived around 3000 BC, making his one of the oldest bodies ever discovered. The axe is the oldest ever found in Europe, and it is complete with its bindings and wooden handle. Apart from the axe, Ötzi was also carrying a flint dagger in a grass sheath, several flints (for lighting fires), and a 6.5-foot- (2-m) long bow with 14 arrows in a deerskin quiver. Searchers also found the remains of a wooden-framed backpack in which he stored his belongings.

Ötzi was wearing these shoes, made of leather and stuffed with grass for warmth.

The copper-headed axe found near Ötzi's body.

11

## BODIES IN THE BOG

*In 1984 first a foot and then the rest of a body were found preserved in a peat bog at Lindow Moss, in Cheshire, England. They belonged to a man who had died over 2,000 years ago. Tests revealed that the man was about 30 years old, with brown hair and a beard. His only clothes were a fur armband and a thong around his neck. Lindow Man, as he became known, seems to have met a violent death, possibly as part of a religious ritual, although no one knows for sure. More than 500 ancient bodies have been found preserved in peat bogs in Europe and North America. The bodies survive in these bogs because in the airless conditions there is no bacteria to break them down.*

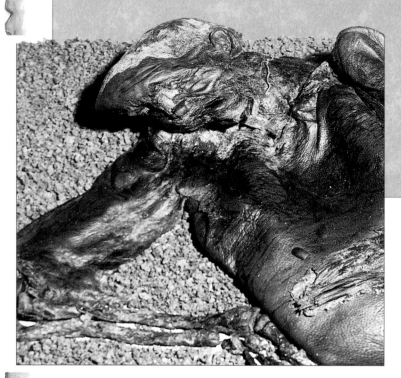

Lindow Man was found in 1984. His throat had been cut, suggesting he was ritually slaughtered.

## Finding out more

What did Ötzi look like? Gradually a more complete picture emerged. He was a man between 25 and 40 years old, and he stood 5 feet (1.5 m) tall, with wavy, dark brown hair and a beard. He was wearing animal-skin clothes, a cape made of braided grass, and leather shoes stuffed with grass for warmth. Around his neck he wore a leather thong threaded through a stone disk, possibly as a lucky charm. A piece of fungus on the end of a string may have been a first-aid kit. Beneath his clothes Ötzi had several mysterious, tattoolike marks—a set of blue lines on his back, a cross behind one knee, and stripes on one ankle. These may have marked him as belonging to a particular tribe, or they may have served some religious purpose.

Scientists are still trying to piece together Ötzi's appearance and lifestyle by studying his body.

## An icy grave

Who was Ötzi and how did he die? Perhaps he was a shepherd, driving his flock down the mountain slopes for the winter. Perhaps he was a hunter, collecting materials for making weapons, or a wandering trader on his way back to his home village. Perhaps he had wandered too far and become lost. A sudden blizzard may have blown up and blocked his path. Overcome by cold, fatigue, and lack of food, he may have decided to rest in the rocky hollow that became his grave. We will never know. Undoubtedly, though, Ötzi is one of the most important finds ever made. He lived between the stone age and the copper age in Europe, at a time when human beings were beginning to use metal for weapons and tools for the first time in their history. The discovery of Ötzi's amazingly well-preserved body, along with his clothes and copper axe, offers us a whole range of new and startling clues about those distant times.

Ötzi may have died while tending his animals, or while making his way home after a trading trip.

## MEGALITHIC TOMBS

*From about 4500 BC, people began to build large, stone monuments over the graves of their dead. These are known as megalithic tombs—megalith means "big stone." They were cavelike structures formed from several huge, upright stone slabs covered by one or more horizontal slabs, called capstones. The stones were originally buried under a mound of earth.*

Megalithic tombs are found all over the world, in Europe, Africa, India, and the Far East.

# CURSE OF THE PHARAOHS

**S**ix months after witnessing the greatest tomb find ever, that of the Egyptian boy king, Tutankhamen, Lord Carnarvon was dead. Officially his death was blamed on blood poisoning caused by an infected mosquito bite. But other more sinister rumors were quick to spread. It is said that at the moment of his death, all the lights in Cairo went out. At the same time, back home in England, Carnarvon's dog howled, then died. Was Carnarvon the first victim of the dreaded pharaoh's curse, the punishment for disturbing the tomb of a king who died over 3,000 years ago?

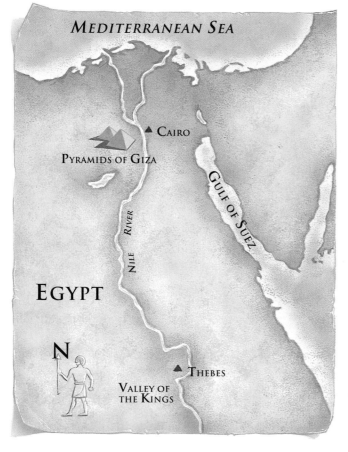

The Valley of the Kings, where Howard Carter made his astonishing discovery, lies in southern Egypt.

## THE START OF THE ADVENTURE

For nearly 20 years, the British archaeologist Howard Carter searched for the tomb of King Tutankhamen, who reigned from 1333 to 1323 BC. Carter was convinced that the tomb lay somewhere in the Valley of the Kings, a desolate valley near Thebes where at least 30 Egyptian pharaohs had been buried.

By 1922, though, time and money were running out. Carter's friends and colleagues were beginning to lose patience with him. But there was still one small patch of ground that Carter had not yet explored. This was close to the tomb of another pharaoh, Ramses IV. Determined to have one last try, Carter persuaded his sponsor, Lord Carnarvon, to finance his efforts once again. Carnarvon agreed, but with a word of warning—there was no more money after this. Carter's obsession had already cost Carnarvon a small fortune.

### A startling discovery

For three days Carter's workmen hacked away at the ground, uncovering the rubble of huts used by the laborers who built Ramses' tomb, but nothing more. Then, on November 6, came the breakthrough they had scarcely dared hope for. Silence greeted Carter as he approached the dig that morning, for the workmen had unearthed a steep flight of steps. The staircase led down to a sealed door bearing the name of Tutankhamen. At once Carter sent a cable to Lord Carnarvon in England:

> AT LAST HAVE MADE WONDERFUL
> DISCOVERY IN VALLEY.
> A MAGNIFICENT TOMB WITH SEALS
> INTACT. RE-COVERED SAME
> FOR YOUR ARRIVAL.
> CONGRATULATIONS

Then, with remarkable restraint, Carter waited for his sponsor to arrive.

King Tutankhamen's exquisite golden death mask.

"Everywhere the glint of gold."

# Wonderful things

Once Lord Carnarvon arrived in Egypt, it took several more days to break through the door and clear the long, rubble-filled passageway behind it. At the end of the passage stood another door. The moment of truth had come at last. With bated breath Carter chipped a small hole in the top left-hand corner, big enough to look through by the light of a candle. What he saw left Carter lost for words. For what seemed like eternity, he could do nothing but stare. "Can you see anything?" Lord Carnarvon asked, unable to bear the suspense any longer. "Yes," replied Carter. "Wonderful things."

Carter later wrote: "At first I could see nothing, the hot air escaping from the chamber causing the candle flame to flicker. But presently, as my eyes grew accustomed to the light, details of the room within emerged slowly from the mist: strange animals, statues, and gold—everywhere the glint of gold."

15

This scarab pendant was one of the many priceless treasures found in Tutankhamen's tomb.

## In Tutankhamen's tomb

Behind the closed door of the tomb lay an extraordinary treasure trove hidden from human eyes for over 3,000 years. The first room that Carter and Carnarvon entered was the outer room of the tomb. According to Egyptian custom, it was filled with precious possessions—chariots, gilded couches, life-sized statues, and an exquisite golden throne.

Each item was very carefully removed and cataloged by Carter and his team before they moved on to the rest of the tomb. The work took several months, and there were still three more chambers to be explored. These were a small wing off the outer room, the main coffin room itself, and a treasure room full of priceless and wonderful burial objects.

## The face of the boy king

On February 17, 1923, Carter at last broke into the burial chamber. He was greeted by what seemed to be a wall of gold. In fact it was the outer casing of a huge golden shrine, inside which there were three more shrines and then a great stone sarcophagus. Within the sarcophagus, Carter found a nest of three coffins, all made in the image of the dead king. The two outer coffins were made of wood and painted in gold leaf. The third coffin was made of solid, 22-carat gold. It was breathtakingly beautiful, and when Carter peered inside, he gazed at last on the mummified body of Tutankhamen himself, his face covered in a fabulous golden death mask inlaid with precious stones. Around the dead king's neck was a garland of lotuses, lilies, and cornflowers—perhaps a last gift from the pharaoh's young queen.

## Curse or coincidence?

In the years that followed the uncovering of Tutankhamen's tomb, several people connected with its discovery died violent or unusual deaths. One was murdered; several committed suicide; one died of pneumonia after catching cold in the tomb. Was this further proof of the power of the pharaoh's curse? It is said that on the day Carter and Carnarvon broke through the door of the antechamber, a sandstorm suddenly blew up, and a hawk, the royal symbol of Ancient Egypt, was seen in the sky—a sign of the dead pharaoh's revenge. One man who dismissed the curse story as nonsense was Howard Carter himself. He died in 1939, at the age of 64, of natural causes.

A funeral procession for an Egyptian pharaoh.

## DEATH AND THE AFTERLIFE IN ANCIENT EGYPT

The Ancient Egyptians were firm believers in life after death and went to great lengths to prepare for the Next World. This was thought to be a happy, carefree land somewhere to the west (it was often called the Kingdom of the West). In order for their souls to reach the Next World, people first had to lead good lives. Then, after death, they had to undergo a series of tests. These included crossing the River of Death, passing through the Twelve Gates that were guarded by serpents, and crossing the Lake of Fire. Next the dead person had to appear before the 42 assessors who read out a long list of sins. The dead person had to swear that he had never committed any of these sins before he could enter the Judgment Hall of Osiris *(see box)*. There the final test took place before the dead person was allowed to enter the Next World.

Tutankhamen's organs were removed and stored in these containers, called canopic jars.

### THE BOOK OF THE DEAD

*The walls of tombs were often decorated with spells, hymns, maps, and prayers, to guide the dead person on the journey to the Next World. These were later written down on papyrus scrolls, known as* The Book of the Dead. *This scene shows the ordeal known as the "Weighing of the Heart." In the Judgment Hall of Osiris, the dead person's heart was weighed against the Feather of Truth. If the person had led a sinful life, his heart would be heavy and tip the scales. It would then be fed to a monster. If the person had led a good life, his heart would balance with the feather, and he could then join his ancestors in the Next World.*

A scene from *The Book of the Dead* showing a dead person's heart being weighed against the Feather of Truth.

## Mummification

The Ancient Egyptians believed that everyone had three souls. These could only survive in the Next World if the body was preserved in a recognizable form. So bodies were mummified to stop them from rotting. The work was carried out by highly skilled embalmers. First, a cut was made in the left side of the corpse, and the intestines, stomach, liver, and lungs were removed and stored in containers. Then, the body was covered with a kind of salt to dry it out. The brain was scooped out through the nose, and the insides of the body were packed with linen or sawdust. The body was smeared with sacred oils and wrapped tightly in bandages, with pieces of jewelry and lucky charms hidden between the layers. The mummy was placed in a coffin. The whole process took about two months to complete.

Anubis was the jackal-headed god of death and embalmers. In his honor, the chief embalmer wore a jackal mask as he went about his work preparing a body for burial.

## Pyramids and tombs

The wealthier the person was, the more elaborate the coffin and tomb. The most elaborate tombs of all were reserved for the pharaohs. At first, pharaohs were buried in huge, pyramid-shaped tombs. Later the Ancient Egyptians buried their pharaohs in underground tombs cut deep into the sides of the valley at Thebes, in an effort to deter grave robbers.

The Egyptians filled their tombs with all the goods and possessions they might need in the Next World. These included food, clothes, and furniture. The tomb walls were lavishly decorated with scenes from everyday life. It was thought that Osiris, the Ruler of the Dead, brought these scenes to life.

Sacred animals, such as cats, were also mummified.

# THE FACE OF AGAMEMNON

From an early age, the German archaeologist Heinrich Schliemann was fascinated by the story of the Trojan War. Schliemann dreamed of finding the site of the ancient city of Troy. In 1873, during a dig at the site where the city was thought to have stood, Schliemann claimed he found the very jewels worn by Helen of Troy (though he was later forced to admit his mistake). Fired by success, he traveled to Mycenae, Greece, to search for the grave of one of the greatest heroes of the story, King Agamemnon.

## QUEST FOR THE KING

The story of the Trojan War is related by the Greek writer Homer in his great epic poem *The Iliad*. According to legend, Agamemnon was ruler of Mycenae, an ancient Greek kingdom that reached the height of its splendor and power in about 1600 BC. Homer tells how Agamemnon led the Greek army to Troy to rescue the beautiful Helen, who had been abducted by a Trojan prince named Paris. At the end of *The Iliad*, after a ten-year siege, Troy is destroyed. Agamemnon's story ends when he returns home, only to be murdered by his wife, Clytemnestra.

Most people believed that Agamemnon was a figure of legend, but not Heinrich Schliemann. A self-made millionaire and a brilliant linguist, he was an ambitious and determined man. He reached Mycenae in August 1876 and began digging just inside the city walls.

1. Lion gate
2. Grave circle
3. Palace
4. Houses

MYCENAE

ISTANBUL

GREECE

AEGEAN SEA

TROY

TURKEY

ATHENS

MYCENAE

HALICARNASSUS

CRETE

MEDITERRANEAN SEA

The Mycenaeans dominated mainland Greece from about 1600–1100 BC. The map also shows the site of Troy.

# The mask of Agamemnon

Schliemann got lucky. Inside a circle of stone slabs, he found five simple shaft graves (a sixth was found later) sunk deep into the ground. From the graves there emerged a dazzling array of exquisite golden objects—goblets and drinking cups, swords, gold vases, crowns, earrings, and necklaces. Alongside this fabulous treasure lay 16 bodies—men, women, and children— their faces covered in golden death masks. One mask in particular caught Schliemann's attention. Its noble features and regal smile convinced him that he had found what he was looking for—the body of Agamemnon. At once he sent a message to the king of Greece, informing him of the discovery. But had he really "gazed upon the face of Agamemnon," as he claimed?

According to legend, Helen of Troy was so beautiful that all the kings of Greece fell in love with her. When she married Menelaus, the kings swore to help him if anyone tried to steal her away.

The fabulous mask of beaten gold that Schliemann believed once covered the dead face of the Mycenean king Agamemnon.

## Schliemann discredited

The graves that Schliemann found became known as Grave Circle A. Schliemann himself had no doubts about the identity of its occupants, but further research proved him wrong. In his haste to remove the treasure, Schliemann destroyed a lot of archaeological evidence. The bodies themselves crumbled to dust when they were exposed to the air. Enough has survived, however, to allow modern scholars to date the grave circle at about 1550 BC, some 300 years before the supposed time of Agamemnon. From the amount of treasure found it is clear that these were royal graves, but some questions remain: Who were these people? Why were so many buried together? We will probably never know.

German archaeologist Heinrich Schliemann (1822–1890). Having made his fortune, he retired from business at the age of 41 in order to devote his life to finding ancient Homeric sites.

An artist's impression of what the mighty Mausoleum of Halicarnassus may have looked like.

## A WONDER OF THE WORLD

*The Mausoleum of Halicarnassus was one of the Seven Wonders of the Ancient World. It was built in 352 BC as a tomb for Mausolus, ruler of Caria in modern-day Turkey. The word "mausoleum" is now used for any large tomb. But from ancient writings, we know that this first mausoleum was a huge, white, rectangular building, standing 131 feet (40 m) high. It had a pyramid-shaped roof with 24 steps leading up to a platform on which stood a marble chariot, pulled by four horses. Soaring above the harbor at Halicarnassus, it was the grandest memorial anyone could hope for. Only fragments of the original Mausoleum remain— Much of the building was destroyed by an earthquake in the 13th century. In the following centuries, the rest was demolished and reused locally as building blocks.*

## THE CATACOMBS OF ROME

*Outside the ancient walls of Rome lies a secret cemetery, a mysterious, underground maze of galleries stretching for 155 miles (250 km). These are the catacombs of Rome, built by early Christians between the 2nd and 4th centuries AD and rediscovered in 1849. Over 750,000 people are buried in graves in these galleries. At that time, it was illegal to bury dead people inside the city walls. But land outside the walls was so expensive that Christians tunneled underground to bury their dead, adding more chambers as the need arose. Some catacombs are six stories deep. The narrow galleries are lined with rows of rectangular slots where the shrouded bodies were placed.*

The central gallery of the catacomb of Priscilla is lined with slots for bodies. The slots were sealed with tiles or stone slabs.

# TOMBS OF THE ROSE CITY

**F**or 1,000 years the legendary city of Petra lay forgotten in the desert hills of Jordan, known only to a few local nomads. Once the fabulous capital of the mighty Nabataean kingdom, it stood at the crossroads of two of the region's most important trade routes. Then, in 1812, a young Swiss explorer, Johann Ludwig Burckhardt, heard rumors of fantastic ruins hidden in the mountains. Could this be Petra at last? Burckhardt was determined to find out . . .

## A ROSE RED CITY

From the age of 20, Johann Burckhardt spent much of his time exploring the Middle East, disguised as a Muslim. He converted to Islam and learned Arabic in preparation for his journeys. In 1812, while traveling from Damascus to Cairo, he heard local people discussing an ancient city hidden in the desert hills. Burkhardt's imagination was gripped. But he needed a good excuse to make a detour from his intended route. He later wrote: "I therefore pretended to have made a vow to have slaughtered a goat in honor of Haroun (Aaron), whose tomb I knew was situated at the extremity of the valley, and by this

The Treasury at Petra, glimpsed from the narrow gorge known as the Siq.

stratagem I thought that I should have the means of seeing the valley on the way to the tomb."

Burckhardt's plan worked. As he followed his guides through a narrow, winding gorge, his excitement grew. Suddenly the hidden city stood before him. Secretly he scribbled notes in a journal concealed under his robes. He managed a quick look at the silent, deserted Treasury building and at the Urn Tomb. But he dared not look closer. His guides were becoming suspicious. If his real intentions were revealed, he would certainly be put to death as a spy. Even this brief glimpse was enough to convince him, however, and he announced to the world that "It seems very probable that the ruins . . . are those of ancient Petra."

# Petra in History

Between the 1st century BC and the 1st century AD, Petra was the capital of the flourishing Nabataean Empire. The Nabataeans were a tough, nomadic people from western Arabia who settled in the region in the 6th century BC. Shepherds by tradition, they soon grew rich by plundering trading caravans. Two important trade routes passed through this region, and the caravans carried rich cargos of gold, spices, copper, incense, and other luxury goods. After the Nabataeans made Petra their capital, it grew into a wealthy and sophisticated city.

The long line of Nabataean kings came to an end in 106 AD when the Romans made the city part of their empire. Petra was still a prosperous city from this time to the early 200s AD. Roman buildings now rose side by side with the Nabataean monuments. However, Petra's importance as a trading center began to decline, and by the 7th century AD, the city had faded into obscurity.

## Tombs in the cliff

Among the most extraordinary monuments at Petra are a series of magnificent royal tombs that were cut into the rose red sandstone of the cliff face. The first is the Urn Tomb, with its facade of great pillars and large tomb-chapel. Dating from the 1st century AD, it was probably the burial place of one of the last of the Nabataean kings. In the 5th century AD, it was converted into a Christian church. Next to it is the Corinthian Tomb, which has been badly worn by the weather, wind and sand erosion, and battered by rock falls. The third tomb is the three-story Palace Tomb, one of the largest monuments in Petra.

## Safe resting place

High up in their cliffside tombs, the bodies of the kings and their courtiers were safe from scavenging animals and greedy grave robbers. According to the Greek writer Strabo (*c.* 63 BC–21 AD), the people of Petra buried their dead rulers with great ceremony.

The magnificent Palace Tomb at Petra.

# ROYAL TOMBS OF CHINA

For centuries scholars heard tales about the elaborate funeral preparations of the emperors of Ancient China. Buried in great luxury, in vast underground tombs, they were laid to rest dressed in magnificent finery and surrounded by fabulous treasures. Then, in 1968 and 1974, two incredible discoveries were made—two royal tombs beyond the scholars' wildest dreams . . .

## AN AMAZING DISCOVERY

In 1974 some workmen were digging a well close to Mount Li, which is near Xi'an in central China. The region had been hit by drought, and water was in short supply. Suddenly their spades struck an underground chamber of wood and earth. As they dug farther, they began to uncover figures of soldiers, larger than life and sculpted from clay. By amazing luck, they had stumbled upon a huge, terra-cotta army. They soon learned that it had been buried more than 2,000 years ago to guard the tomb of China's first emperor, Shi Huangdi. The tomb itself lies close by, under a burial mound covered in apricot trees, but it has yet to be excavated and explored.

The kneeling figure of an archer. The soldiers in the terra-cotta army once carried real weapons.

### The terra-cotta army

Further excavations revealed an army of 6,000 soldiers —infantry, archers, horsemen, and charioteers—in battle formation, ready to defend the tomb. The clay figures had once held real bronze swords, spears, and crossbows in their hands, and the charioteers had driven real wooden chariots. No two faces were the same. Experts believe each had been modeled on the face of a real-life soldier in the emperor's army. Traces of colors show that the figures were once brightly painted in green, purple, and yellow. The soldiers stood in a huge pit. Two more pits were later discovered, bringing the total army to 10,000 st___ng.

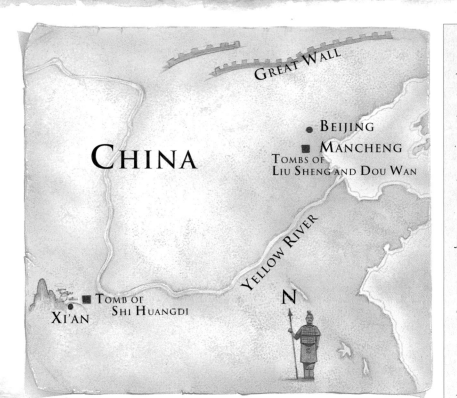

## THE EMPEROR'S TOMB

*An extraordinary description of the emperor's tomb has survived, written by the Chinese historian Si-ma Qian (145–c. 90 BC):*

*"As soon as the First Emperor became king of Qin, work was begun on his mausoleum at Mount Li. More than 700,000 conscripts . . . labored there. They dug through three underground streams; they poured molten copper for the outer coffin; and they filled the burial chamber with models of palaces, pavilions and official buildings, as well as fine utensils, precious stones and rarities . . . The waterways of the empire, the Yellow and Yangtze rivers, and even the great ocean itself, were represented by mercury and were made to flow mechanically. Above, the heavenly constellations were depicted, while below a representation of the earth. Lamps using whale oil were installed to burn for a long time."*

The terra-cotta army guarded the emperor's tomb for more than 2,000 years.

## A tomb fit for an emperor

The tomb guarded by the terra-cotta army belonged to Shi Huangdi, the first emperor of China. In 247 BC, at just 13 years of age, Shi Huangdi became king of Qin, one of the many independent states that made up China. Soon after this Shi Huangdi began to conquer neighboring states, establishing his capital near the present-day city of Xi'an.

Shi Huangdi also began preparations for the building of his tomb. Some 700,000 laborers were put to work. The tomb took 36 years to build, and it was said to resemble an underground city, with a throne room, treasury, walls, gates, and watch towers. To keep the tomb's whereabouts a secret, the workmen were killed and buried inside it. There were booby traps to deter grave robbers, including crossbows that were primed and ready to fire at intruders. Finally the tomb was covered with earth and planted with trees to make it look like an

ordinary hill. Despite these elaborate precautions, within three years of Shi Huangdi's death, his tomb was plundered by a rebel army who set the pits on fire, burying the clay army in ash and mud. Ironically, it was this layer of ash and mud that preserved the figures until their discovery in 1974.

Life-sized models of horses and horse-drawn chariots were buried with the soldiers.

## Search for eternal life

Shi Huangdi was a powerful and ruthless leader. Until the discovery of the terra-cotta army, he was probably best remembered as the builder of the Great Wall, constructed to keep his enemies out. Despite his fierce and warlike behavior, one thing terrified Shi Huangdi—death. He lived in constant fear of assassination, and several attempts were made on his life. To safeguard him and to try to predict his future, he employed 300 court astrologers. He also spent a fortune searching for a magic potion that would give him eternal life. He sent out an expedition to a legendary island off China's coast where the potion was said to be brewed. The expedition never returned. In 210 BC, while touring the eastern provinces, the emperor died. He was just 49 years old.

Emperor Shi Huangdi (260–210 BC), the first emperor of China.

## DEATH OF THE EMPEROR

*A strange story surrounds the death of Emperor Shi Huangdi. His ministers tried to keep his death a secret while they planned for the succession of the next emperor. They managed to return his body to the capital by covered carriage, acting as if the emperor were still alive. They took the dead emperor food and drink, and issued royal commands as usual. But it was summer, and the body soon began to smell. To disguise the stench, the councilors arranged for a cartload of rotten fish to follow the royal carriage wherever it went. No one asked why—nobody dared!*

The imperial carriage makes its way to the capital.

29

## THE JADE PRINCE AND PRINCESS

In 1968 Chinese soldiers on exercises at Mancheng, about 68 miles (110 km) to the southwest of Beijing, made an extraordinary discovery—two huge, manmade caves full of treasures, hollowed out of the rocky hillside. These were the tombs of a prince and princess of the Han dynasty, Liu Sheng and Dou Wan. Prince Liu Sheng ruled over the province of Chung Shun, near Beijing, and died in about 113 BC. His wife, Princess Dou Wan, died about 12 years later. Both were buried with all the things they would need in the afterlife—food and wine, fine silks, thousands of precious vases, lamps, jade, and gold ornaments, and plates and cups of silver and gold. In the prince's tomb, archaeologists also found carriages and the bodies of 16 horses and 11 dogs.

## Burial suits

The most spectacular treasures found were the two priceless jade suits in which the prince and princess had been buried, the first of their kind to be discovered. Each was made from thousands of tiny pieces of highly polished jade, sewn together with gold thread. The right to be buried in a jade suit was a great honor, reserved only for members of the royal family. The prince's suit was about 6 feet (2m) long and made of 2,498 jade pieces. The princess's suit was 5 feet 6 inches (1.7 m) long and made of 2,160 jade pieces. Each suit had taken a team of highly skilled craftspeople over ten years to make.

## The power of jade

In Ancient China jade was a symbol of power and purity. Because it was so hard, it was thought to be able to prevent bodies from decaying after death. This is why the burial suits of the prince and princess were made of jade. Unfortunately, when the tombs were opened, there was little trace of the two bodies—they had long since disintegrated into dust, and the jade suits crumbled into pieces. The suits have now been restored to their former stunning glory.

Two jade tokens from the royal tombs.

The jade funeral suit of Princess Dou Wan. It was made in 12 sections, stitched together with gold thread.

## RECENT DISCOVERIES

*More ancient tombs are still being discovered in China. But one tomb continues to baffle archaeologists—that of the first Ming emperor who ruled from 1368 to 1398. It is known that the tombs of several Ming emperors lie somewhere near Beijing, but the first emperor was careful to leave no clues behind. He had 13 coffins and 13 tombs ready for when he died. After his death, each coffin was buried with fitting pomp and splendor so that no one knew which tomb contained his body and his precious store of treasures!*

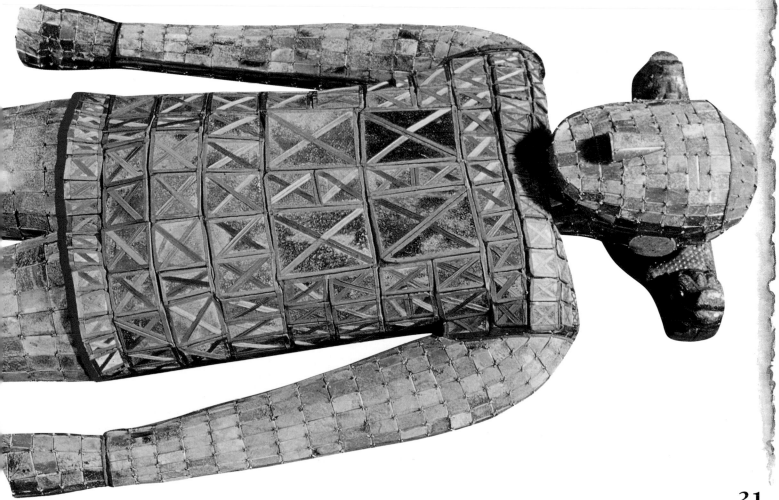

Two of the four bronze and silver leopards found in Princess Dou Wan's tomb.

# SHIP GRAVES

Burial places come in many shapes and sizes—from the pyramids of Ancient Egypt to the underground catacombs of Rome. The grandest graves have always belonged to the richest and most powerful people, and the Vikings were no exception. Kings, queens, and great Viking chieftains were buried in longships—the greatest status symbol of seafaring people. Much of our knowledge of the Vikings comes from two burial ships discovered at Gokstad and Oseberg, in Norway.

The location of the ship graves.

## THE OSEBERG SHIP

In 1903 farmworkers digging into a grassy mound on the river plain at Oseberg, Norway, made an astonishing discovery—the remains of an ancient longship buried more than 1,000 years before. Reports of the find soon reached the University of Oslo, and a team of archaeologists arrived to continue the excavations. They were about to unearth the richest ship grave ever discovered.

Despite the passage of time and the damage caused by medieval grave robbers, the clay soil around the sleek wooden ship had preserved it and its contents remarkably well. The archaeologists found not only a huge collection of wooden furniture *(see box),* but also walnuts, oats, wheat, wild apples, herbs, and spices. The grave's owner was not meant to go hungry in the next world.

## A grave for a Viking queen

In a burial chamber at the back of the ship, the excavators found the remains of two bodies. Both were women, one elderly, the other in her late twenties and, judging by the splendor of her burial, of royal birth. She may have been Queen Asa, grandmother of Harald Finehair, who ruled Norway in the 9th century AD. The older woman may have been her maid, sacrificed and buried with her mistress to look after her in the afterlife.

### GRAVE FURNITURE

*The Vikings buried their dead with everything they might need in the next world—food, weapons, furniture, personal belongings, even horses and slaves. Among the wealth of grave goods found in the Oseberg ship was a large collection of wooden objects, including beds, four horse-drawn sleighs, a four-wheeled cart, chests, boxes, and a chair. The skeletons of at least ten horses lay nearby. There were also five wooden posts with their tops exquisitely carved into snarling animal heads. It is not certain what these strange posts were used for.*

One of the five animal-head posts found in the Oseberg ship.

The restored Oseberg ship is now on display in a museum near Oslo, Norway.

A Viking ship burial. The Vikings believed that the ship would carry the dead person safely into the next world, complete with the belongings, and even the companions, they would need there.

# THE STORY OF SUTTON HOO

In May 1939 a team of archaeologists began work on a series of 16 ancient burial mounds at Sutton Hoo, Suffolk, England. The site lay in grounds owned by Mrs. Edith Pretty, who had been told that they were probably made by the Anglo-Saxons after their invasion of England in the 7th century AD. The largest mound was 98 feet (30 m) long, 75 feet (23 m) wide, and almost 10 feet (3 m) high. As the archaeologists dug, they began to unearth clumps of rusty nails known as "clench nails" because of their shape. These were vital and intriguing clues. They indicated that the mound covered a ship grave, the traditional Anglo-Saxon way of burying a king.

## The Sutton Hoo ship

Working with extreme care, the archaeologists removed the earth to reveal the outlines of an enormous ship. The wood had decayed long before, but the impression of the ship remained in the sandy soil. It was 88 feet (27 m) long by 13 feet (4 m) wide—a huge boat once propelled by 14 oarsmen. It had been hauled up from the river to its final resting place for a solemn funeral ceremony.

## Tomb or memorial?

In the center of the ship was a burial chamber that contained a wealth of amazing and priceless objects. The items included beautiful gold and garnet jewelry, silver bowls, cups, and spoons, drinking horns, lamps, a lyre, combs, leather shoes, and fragments of fine clothes. They were laid out as if they had been arranged around a body. But there was no body to be found. Perhaps the ship and its precious contents formed part of a memorial to a mighty leader killed far away?

One of two shoulder clasps from Sutton Hoo, made of gold inlaid with enamel. They once fastened the king's armor.

King Raedwald leads his warriors into battle. Is this the king whose burial chamber was found at Sutton Hoo?

## Clues to a warrior king?

The objects found inside the burial chamber pointed to the wealth and power of the man for whom it was built. Judging by the magnificent helmet, shield, sword, and scepter found in the grave, he must certainly have been a king and a great warrior. But which king was he? Two small silver spoons engraved with Christian symbols suggest that he might have been King Raedwald, ruler of East Anglia. He died in about 625 AD. But some of the gold coins found in the ship were not made until many years later. Other suggestions include Ecgric, the heroic brother of King Anna, one of Raedwald's successors, or King Aethelhere, Anna's heir. Aethelhere's body was lost at sea off the coast of Northumberland. His ship may have been buried in his memory. All we know for sure is that the ship must have belonged to one of the Anglo-Saxon kings who ruled eastern England from their camp at Rendlesham, just a few miles from Sutton Hoo.

The reconstructed Sutton Hoo helmet, decorated with iron and bronze, fit for a king.

# THE MASK OF THE MAYA

The mysterious Temple of Inscriptions in Palenque, Mexico.

**B**efore the arrival of European conquistadors (conquerors) in the 15th and 16th centuries, many wealthy and sophisticated civilizations flourished in the Americas. From about 250–900 AD, the Maya held sway over southern Mexico. Their empire was divided into cities, each governed by a noble and powerful ruler. With the eventual decline of the Maya in the 1500s, these spectacular cities were abandoned to the forest, and later, to the hands of archaeologists, anxious to unravel their secrets . . .

## THE DAY OF THE DEAD

*Mexico's most fantastic festival is the Day of the Dead, celebrated each year on November 2. With its origins stretching back to the 3rd century AD, it is the day on which the spirits of the dead are believed to return briefly to the land of the living. Since their visit is so short, the spirits must be given a good welcome. People hold feasts in their honor and take picnics to the cemetery so they can talk with and sing to their dead relations. Children buy sugar skulls, chocolate coffins, and skeletons of bread!*

Sugar skulls are exchanged as presents on the Day of the Dead.

## A SECRET STAIRCASE

In 1949 the Mexican archaeologist Alberto Ruz was excavating the ruins of the Temple of Inscriptions in the ancient Mayan city of Palenque. There he made an amazing discovery—the first few steps of a mysterious staircase leading deep down inside the temple pyramid. It took three years for Ruz and his colleagues to clear the rubble off the steps. At last, with great dread, they crept through the passage at the bottom of the staircase. Two walls had been built across the passage. Behind the first wall they found a small stone box containing three pottery dishes, three seashells, several jade beads, and a beautiful tear-shaped pearl. Beyond the second wall they discovered the smashed bones of six young men and women who had probably been sacrificed by the temple priests. But the greatest find was yet to come . . .

The extent of the Aztec, Maya, and Inca empires, and the area of the Moche culture.

NORWAY

N

PALENQUE

ATLANTIC OCEAN

PACIFIC OCEAN

MOCHE AD 100-600

AZTEC AD 1200-1521

MAYA EMPIRE AD 250-900

INCA EMPIRE AD 1438-1534

## INCA MUMMIES

*Like the Ancient Egyptians, the Incas of Peru mummified the corpses of their dead rulers. The body of the Sapa Inca, or emperor, was dressed in rich clothes, with a golden death mask placed over its face to protect it from the dangers of the afterlife. At festival times the mummy was paraded through the city streets and honored with prayers and sacrifices. At other times the mummy was looked after in the royal palace almost as if it were still alive. The mummies of past emperors were often consulted in important matters of state, with special seats reserved for them at council meetings.*

The mummified body of the emperor is paraded through the streets.

## Pacal the Great

At the end of the passage, the way was blocked by a huge, triangular stone. The slab was sealed tight all the way around except for a small hole in one corner. When Ruz peered through, he saw an enormous room. The walls of the room were covered with carvings. In the center of the room was a large, elaborately carved, rectangular stone slab.

On June 15, 1952, Ruz and his colleagues lifted the stone slab. Beneath it they found a large tomb containing the skeleton of the ancient Lord of Palenque, Pacal the Great, ruler of the city from 613–83 AD. Nothing remained of the rich robes in which he had been buried apart from red powder and dust. But the fabulous jewelry that had adorned Pacal's body was still in place. Most amazing of all was the exquisite death mask that covered his face— a life-sized mosaic of more than 200 pieces of jade, with eyes of shell and obsidian. Pacal also had jade rings on his fingers, jade discs in his ears, and a necklace of 18 jade beads. A piece of jade had been placed in each hand and another in his mouth. At his feet lay huge, pearl-shaped pieces of jade and a jade figure of the sun god.

Jade was the Maya's most precious stone, a symbol of life itself and more valuable even than gold. In Mayan times the jade surrounding Pacal's body was considered a fitting tribute to the mightiest of Palenque's rulers. For Ruz and his colleagues, it was a treasure trove beyond their wildest dreams.

The stone slab that covered the tomb of Pacal the Great, Lord of Palenque.

Pacal's jade burial mask that Ruz found deep underneath the Temple of Inscriptions.

## THE LORDS OF SIPAN

In 1987 a number of rare and precious items of gold and silver mysteriously appeared for sale in Peru. The police called in an archaeologist, William Alva, to help in their investigations. He discovered that the treasure had been stolen from an ancient pyramid tomb in the village of Sipan—the tomb of a mighty warrior-priest. The priest belonged to the Moche, a group of farmers who lived along the northern coast of Peru from about 100 to 600 AD. He was not buried alone. Apart from the priceless treasures found in the tomb, there were several other bodies—five people and a dog. The tomb of an older warrior-priest was also found in the pyramid.

As well as being farmers, the Moche were fierce warriors. Warrior-priests presided over religious ceremonies, such as sacrifices and burials.

The burial chamber of the Lord of Sipan and his companions.

39

# UNSOLVED MYSTERIES

Whenever an ancient tomb is found, news of its discovery hits the headlines, and the questions begin. Whom did the tomb belong to? When was it made? Does it contain a body or a fabulous trove of treasure? Of course, not every tomb can be identified. Many are shrouded in mystery and will always remain so. Here are just a few stories of tombs that have yet to be identified or found . . .

## WINTER SUNLIGHT

After five years of excavating and restorating, the Irish archaeologist Michael O'Kelly stood in the dark chamber inside the prehistoric grave at Newgrange, in northeastern Ireland, and waited. It was December 21, 1969, the winter solstice, and the shortest day of the year. Just before 9 A.M., Professor O'Kelly's patience was rewarded. As the sun rose, a beam of light shone through a hole in the roof and illuminated the chamber in which he stood. He was witnessing a scene observed many times by the builders of Newgrange, 5,000 years ago.

Deep inside the grave at Newgrange, Michael O'Kelly witnessed an amazing scene.

On the shortest day of every year, a beam of sunlight shines directly into the burial chamber of the tomb at Newgrange.

Chamber

Mound

Passage

Hole in roof

Beam of sunlight

This carved stone marks the entrance to Newgrange.

## High kings of Tara

Legend says that Newgrange was the burial place of the Irish high kings of Tara, which lies 12 miles (20 km) to the southwest. It is said that one of these kings, Cormac mac Airt, gave strict orders not to be buried in the mound. But his servants ignored his orders and carried his body to Newgrange. As they reached the Boyne River, the corpse swelled to three times its normal size, making a crossing impossible. So Cormac was buried in the river bank opposite Newgrange, just as he had wished.

## Newgrange—tomb or timekeeper?

Like Stonehenge in England, Newgrange seems to have been built as a kind of calendar. The beam of light that shines directly into the tomb marks the shortest day of the year and announces the start of a new one as the days begin to lengthen. But Newgrange is also a prehistoric grave—one of the finest in Europe. The saucer-shaped mound around the grave is constructed of thousands of round stones and turf. Inside the mound is a narrow passage, 3.3 feet (1 m) wide and 69 feet (21 m) long. The passage is lined with slabs of stone and leads into a chamber. Here archaeologists have found human bones plus beads, pendants, and a bone chisel, all of which were probably left as funeral offerings. However, the identity of the mound's occupants remains a mystery.

## THE MYSTERY OF SILBURY HILL

*In the rolling countryside of Wiltshire, England, stands a huge, humanmade mound, some 131 feet (40 m) high and covering an area of over 5 acres. This is Silbury Hill, built about 4,500 years ago. Local legends say that a life-sized golden figure, a king in a golden coffin, or a man on horseback dressed in golden armor lies buried in the hill. But there is no evidence that the hill was even intended as a burial site. So why was such an enormous mound built? So far this mystery has yet to be solved.*

# THE GRAVE OF KING ARTHUR

The famous story of King Arthur and the Knights of the Round Table is a mystery in itself. Did a King Arthur ever actually exist? Where was Camelot, his royal court, and castle? And if he did exist, where was he buried? It is possible that King Arthur was a real historical figure, an early leader of the Britons who led his knights against Saxon invaders in the 5th century AD. There are also many suggestions about where in England Camelot might have been situated—from North Wales to Cornwall to Somerset, in England.

According to legend, when Arthur died, his body was taken to a mythical resting place, the Isle of Avalon. But if Arthur was a real historical figure, where is his earthly grave? In the 12th century AD, as he passed through Wales, King Henry II heard a rumor about the location of Arthur's grave—it lay between two pillars in the old church at Glastonbury Abbey, in Somerset. But before King Henry could investigate the rumor, disaster struck. Fire swept through the abbey and destroyed it. Henry gave orders for the church to be rebuilt, but he died in 1189, the year before a very exciting discovery was made.

The ruins of Glastonbury Abbey, Somerset, England.

Legend says that King Arthur was fatally wounded by his evil nephew Mordred and died shortly afterward. Then his body was taken to the mythical Isle of Avalon.

## Arthur's bones?

On his deathbed, a monk of the abbey asked to be buried between the same two pillars of the old church. The abbey authorities hesitated, but only briefly. They knew that if they found Arthur's remains, they would be able to attract more pilgrims and raise more funds. So they began digging between the two pillars. Soon they unearthed a stone slab inscribed with a cross and these words:

HIC IACET SEPULTUS INCLITUS REX ARTURIUS IN INSULA AVALONIA
*HERE LIES BURIED THE RENOWNED KING ARTHUR IN THE ISLE OF AVALON*

Digging deeper they discovered a hollow oak log used as a coffin and full of bones. The skull bore the marks of a great gaping wound, which supported the story of King Arthur's death in battle. Clinging to another set of bones were strands of long, fair hair. Were these the bones of Guinevere, Arthur's beautiful queen?

## A trick for the tourists

All of this is based on hearsay. No one knows if such a coffin was, in fact, ever found. The whole story might have been a hoax invented by the monks to attract pilgrims who would supply the much-needed funds for the abbey. The bones were only shown to a few select visitors and were not put on public display as one might expect. There is evidence, however, that the cross and inscription did exist. So the mystery thickens. Some scholars believe that the cross could have dated from Arthur's time; others are doubtful. Unfortunately the cross itself has long since vanished without a trace. It seems likely that the monks did excavate an ancient grave in the abbey. But was it King Arthur's? We probably won't ever know.

## IN SEARCH OF ALEXANDER

*When he died of a fever in 323 BC, Alexander the Great was just 33 years old. In 13 short years he had created the greatest empire ever, stretching from Greece in the west to India in the east. After his death in Babylon, Alexander's body was embalmed. It then remained in the city for two years while workmen completed a fabulous funeral chariot to carry it in state back home to Macedonia (in northeastern Greece). Alexander was to lie in a golden coffin with a golden lid, under a pillared canopy, decorated with carvings and paintings of his greatest victories. However, as the chariot passed through Egypt, it was waylaid and put on display, first in Memphis, then in Alexandria. There it remained for 300 years. After that Alexander's body was never seen again. Neither a tomb nor any remains were ever found at Alexandria. If his tomb is ever discovered, one of the greatest mysteries of the ancient world will have been solved.*

43

# GLOSSARY

**archaeologist**  A person who studies human history by examining remains and ruins such as burial sites and ancient cities.

**astrologer**  Someone who observes the stars and planets and interprets how they affect people's lives.

**bacteria**  Tiny, one-celled organisms that can cause decay and disease.

**catacombs**  Underground cemeteries.

**conquistadors**  The Spanish conquerors who invaded Mexico and Peru in the 16th century.

**cremation**  The burning of a dead body.

**embalmer**  Someone who treats a dead body with oils or other substances to prevent it from decaying.

**facade**  The front of a building.

**jade**  A hard, semiprecious green stone, highly prized by many ancient peoples.

**mausoleum**  A magnificent tomb.

**megalithic tomb**  An ancient tomb constructed from large stones.

**mummification**  The Ancient Egyptian method of embalming a dead body and wrapping it in bandages.

**nomad**  A person who wanders from place to place, instead of settling down to live in one place.

**obsidian**  A dark, shiny, volcanic rock that looks like glass.

**pharaoh**  The title given to the king of Ancient Egypt.

**pyre**  A large fire for cremating (burning) a dead body.

**sarcophagus**  A stone coffin usually decorated with sculptures and inscriptions.

**terra-cotta**  A brownish red clay.

# FURTHER READING

Baquedano, Elizabeth. *Aztec, Inca, and Maya.* Knopf Young
   Readers, 1993

Bendick, Jeanne. *Egyptian Tombs.* Watts, 1989

Bendick, Jeanne. *Tombs of the Ancient Americas.* Watts, 1993

Berrill, Margaret. *Mummies, Masks, and Mourners.* Dutton, 1990

Clare, John D., ed. *Vikings* (Living History Series). HarBrace, 1992

Edmondson, Elizabeth. *The Trojan War.* Simon & Schuster Childrens, 1992

Gold, Susan Dudley. *The Pharaohs' Curse.* Crestwood, 1990

Greene, Jacqueline D. *The Maya.* Watts, 1992

Hook, Jason. *The Vikings.* Thomson Learning, 1993

Hooper-Trout, Lawana. *The Maya* (Indians of North America Series)
   Chelsea House, 1991

Lazo, Caroline. *The Terra-Cotta Army of Emperor Qin.* Simon &
   Schuster Childrens, 1993

LeSueur, Meridel. *The Mound Builders.* Watts, 1974

Margeson, Sue. *Viking.* Knopf Young Readers, 1994

Meyer, Carolyn and Gallenkamp, Charles. *The Mystery of the
   Ancient Maya,* rev. ed., Simon & Schuster Childrens, 1994

Morley, Jacqueline. *An Egyptian Pyramid.* Bedrick Books, 1993

O'Neal, Michael. *Pyramids: Opposing Viewpoints.* Lucent, 1994

Putnam, James. *Pyramid* (Eyewitness Books). Knopf Young Readers, 1994

# INDEX